A
BLACK MAN
FOLLOWING
A JEWISH
MESSIAH

MORRIS GRAVES, JR

LIVE ON IMPACT MEDIA

I challenged Morris, as a black Christian, to examine the Jew and Israel from a biblical point of view. He did and it changed his life.

I promise you that Morris' book will change YOUR life!

SID ROTH
HOST, IT'S SUPERNATURAL! TV PROGRAM

A Black Man Following A Jewish Messiah

Author Morris Graves, Jr.

Copyright © Morris Graves Jr.

For more information on Morris Graves Jr.:
please visit: www.morrisgravesjr.com

ISBN: 979-8-9911638-0-4

Library of Congress Control Number: 2024916173

Published in the United States by:
Live On Impact Media
www.liveonimpactmedia.com

Printed in the United States of America First Edition
1 2 3 4 5 6 7 8 9 10

Regarding that which
I bring to the body of Messiah,
My pigmentation is irrelevant

DRAWING BY MORRIS GRAVES, JR

CONTENTS

INTRODUCTION -
JOURNEY TO SANCTIFICATION

In Philippians 1:6, Paul writes this incredible statement: "I am certain of this, that He who began a good work in you will be faithful to complete it at the day of Jesus Messiah." This embodies the phrase "journey to sanctification." We are all a work in progress, and God is the only one who can bring us to that place of perfection. God has set us apart—sanctified us—to live a life, a journey, of representing Jesus to a lost and dying world.

If you have been born again, then perhaps you are aware of the struggle to be well-pleasing to God. This is the story of my journey to wholeness. This is the story of how the Holy Spirit brought me face to face with my own humanity and empowered me to see the church and the world through His eyes. I pray that it will inspire you to view yourself and the world through the loving eyes of a Jewish Messiah.

After only five days of sharing a jail cell with three other men, I gave my life to Jesus. In a   moment of desperation, I had turned to my grandmother's God. I had called on a God that before now, I believed wanted nothing to do with me. Like little ghouls, tormenting thoughts, images of what I had done, and scenarios of the worst kind regarding the fate of my wife and son raced through my mind.

I knew nothing about Christianity. In fact, because of childhood experiences, I had absolutely no desire to even investigate it. But it is those moments of despair that render the heart vulnerable.

The vulnerable become the needy, and the needy are open to the most irrational solutions. Before this moment, I believed there was no greater absurdity than Christianity. Sitting in that cell, keenly aware of my own helplessness, I had come face to face with my worst enemy.

I'm not certain if I had ever actually hated myself. But now, facing the reality of the devastation I had caused, the dark future looming over me like a bad storm, I had never hated anyone more.

All I wanted was to put distance between the man I was, and the man I wanted to be. What was once a seed that my grandmother had planted in me years before, was now budding. It came as one of those sudden moments, a seemingly random thought. The small Gideon Bible that I held in my hand, it could change me. God was clearly tossing me a lifeline.

It was hard to believe that only four months had passed since the night I sat on that grassy lawn with my legs folded, my feet tucked under my thighs, gun in my lap, waiting for the police to come.

I was still too violently angry to entertain regret for what I had just done, too inebriated to consider the lives I had destroyed only moments ago. I truly believed that I had only wounded him. I was totally oblivious to the reality that I would be facing murder charges within hours.

I could still feel the surge of adrenaline pulsating within me. The raging beast, fueled by an emotional cocktail of rage, fear, pride, and arrogance, tuned out the deafening wailing all around me. Oddly enough, I can't remember what I was contemplating as I sat there.

I think as reality began to seep in, my mind, my entire body just went numb. My life, as I had known it, was over. His wife, his children, my wife, my children. We would all spend the rest of our lives trying to crawl from beneath the traumatizing rubble left behind by a rage-filled drunken coward.

This was not a bad dream. I would not wake up and breathe a sigh of relief, realizing this was all a nightmare. This was a culmination of my lived experiences as a Black man in America, and I had come unraveled at the seams like a poorly stitched hem.

Four months later, having taken a plea bargain, and sentenced to fifteen years for second-degree murder, I found myself confined to a prison dormitory in a maximum-security prison. I sat on a bunk, my head down, chin pressed against my chest. My legs folded, feet tucked under my thighs, a Bible resting in my lap. I could feel the adrenaline racing through my nervous system. I had been in a processing dormitory for two weeks.

A bottom bunk was now my home. I had not said one word to the visibly terrified man bunking only three feet across from me. We had made eye contact maybe three times. Each time, his look, his posture, seemed to be awaiting the inevitable. Each time, I felt a strange sense of compassion for him.

It had been a span of no more than 15 minutes since the desk officer had ordered my neighbor to go to the back and take a much-needed shower. A nervous tension came over me as I watched the desk officer leave the dormitory for the first time since I had been there. Three inmates entered immediately after the officer's departure. I did not look at their faces as they passed me and proceeded to the shower room.

I struggled to resist the images that were flooding

my mind, created by the sound of the shower, of flesh being pounded, of muffled dialogue and groanings. The three men exited as quietly as they had come in.

By now I was only pretending to read the Bible, and I could hear him struggling to make his way back and finally rest on his bunk. I was ashamed to look up. Was he sitting there staring at me? Should I have jeopardized my own well-being by coming to his aid? Somewhere within me, I believed it would have been the Christian thing to do. I could feel his eyes locked on me.

Where was this mass of shame and guilt coming from? He was a child molester, I repeated to myself. He deserved what had just happened to him. These thoughts brought me no comfort. Why was I feeling this flood of compassion for a White man?

As a baby boomer, born in the South, I had seen first-hand the disdain that White people held for me, and I held equally for them. These feelings were foreign to me. Finally, I could not take it anymore. I slowly begin to raise my head anticipating making eye contact with this morbidly obese, foul smelling, pitiful man.

Without exchanging a word his eyes communicated to me. You're sitting there reading that Bible, and you let them do this to me. I could only imagine what he was interpreting in my eyes, what my facial expression must have been communicating. My eyes returned to the pages of the Bible. I could hear him breathing. My heart was hurting for him.

I was confused. Why was I feeling this way? Maybe it was because of the pain I had caused to others only months before. Or perhaps, could it be that I was experiencing the transforming power of the new birth? I had been immersed in the pages of the Bible, so much so, that I had begun to inject myself into the text. The Bible had become a means of escaping the chaos of prison life. I would be on the battlefield fighting epic wars with King David. Walking along the shores of the sea of Galilee gripped by every word that came out of Jesus' mouth. Abraham, Ezekiel, Isaiah, Ezra, Samuel, James, Peter, John, and Paul, these men had fast become my friends.

In retrospect it's now crystal clear, as to why I had this overwhelming compassion. The God of the Bible had become my God, His only begotten Son had become my Messiah. I was now just a man with the deep desire to know Jesus.

However, unbeknownst to me, the journey that brought me to this place would be filled with harrowing tales of encounters with individuals, from my childhood into my adult life, as far back as I can remember, the journey that brought me to this moment was filled with harrowing tales of encounters with people struggling to meet their own needs at my expense. I was the oldest of six children in a single-parent home.

My mother worked very hard to make sure our essential needs were met. As a child, I remember being envious of my friends because they would receive government food at the beginning of the month: large cans of pulled chicken, blocks of cheese, canned peanut butter, and bags of prunes. In my small mind, they were far better off than we were. I once asked my mother why we didn't get government food. I don't remember what she was doing, but I do remember her response. She turned to me and said, "Morris, nothing pushes you down harder than a handout."

My mother modeled a strong work ethic, yet she failed to factor in the dangers of leaving her children in the care of emotionally impoverished people. At some point, we all have had our minds, or our bodies, and in most cases, both, trespassed upon by someone who represented authority, security, and love. When a child is subjected to adult-inflicted perversion, that level of trauma is mentally devastating.

The child is incapable of processing what they have experienced. They instinctively know it's wrong and evil. For most children, it is easier to suppress it deep into the subconscious and act as if nothing has happened rather than telling someone. The result is a grossly distorted image of God being formed inside the child, which was my case. I would continue to grapple with my identity and my sense of unworthiness, feeling emotionally unfulfilled.

That all changed when I accepted Jesus, the Jewish Messiah, as my Savior. I asked God to forgive me for my sins and invited the Holy Spirit to live within me. It was from that very moment that I embarked on my journey to sanctification.

PREFACE

An authentic Christ encounter will awaken the spirit of a man. A fully alert spirit, will naturally seek the heart of God as a bounty. The pursuit of God both sustains and changes man. The old nature is not improved but removed. Those engulfed in the genuine love of God, the Agape, recognize no boundaries, be it ethnic, cultural, social or otherwise.

There is no beauty more splendid in comparison to the love of God illuminating from the body of Messiah. Those who follow this Jewish Messiah give no credence to, "foolish controversies and genealogies." Strife and disputes about the law are recognized as, "unprofitable and worthless."

In reference to this Jewish Messiah, there is a verse in the Bible, St. John 12:19 which states, "The whole world has gone after him!" Yeshua, then and now, is offering humanity the opportunity to become the people God intended them to be.

For the first time in my life, as a Black man following a Jewish Messiah, I feel as if I am doing the reasonable thing. Ironically, as I relax the grip that clings to my old nature, losing myself in my longing to discover more of Yeshua, I am slowly coming to terms with the man God created me to be. I exist for His glory.

Yeshua made this powerful statement to God in John 17:4, "I have brought you glory on earth by finishing the work you gave me to do." In searching the sacred passages, I find that this is the only way we can bring true glory to God. I desire to make the exact declaration to the God of all glory when my own life and service draws to its conclusion.

On a personal level, my prayer is that I consistently yield to the leadership of the Holy Spirit. I believe there is no alternative to truly pursuing Messiah-likeness, which is what we call being a Christian. If the Holy Spirit is not your guide, you are venturing down the wrong path. You may become a better version of yourself, however, the best version of a man is a far cry from having the heart of Yeshua.

The first step towards pursuing Messiah-likeness is dying to self-reliance. The word of God declares us no longer Jew, Gentile, slave nor free, neither male nor female. Those born again find their identity in the Holy Spirit's leadership. He guides them down a road specifically designed to fashion each of us into the individuals we were created to be. Only then, can we perfectly reflect the mind of the Messiah.

If we are truly one in the Messiah, we cannot be products of uniformity. We are like a fingerprint, each one possessing its own unique design. When my unique design succumbs to uniformity, it is at that point I have abandoned God's original plan for my life.

As a member of the body of Messiah, my prayer is that we all may recognize the great cultural divide and commit to being bridge builders. The visible barriers that impede unity amongst our ranks, as passive as they may be, are hurdles the Church has yet to clear. I believe denominations subsequently protect themselves from cultural invasion by demanding their parishioners to adhere with their own beliefs and practices.

The very core of Yeshua's teachings challenges us to surrender to His indwelling presence, and to allow the Holy Spirit to put Messiah's life on display through us. The alternative is to imitate His life in our own strength. History has proven the alternative produces disastrous results. I am not advocating abandoning discipline.

Those that have truly surrendered to the Holy Spirit are amongst the most disciplined people in the world. Their verbiage and conduct reflect the instructions of the Holy Spirit as well as the sayings of Yeshua according to John 14:26, "But the Helper, the Holy Spirit, whom the Father will send in My name, He will teach you all things, and bring to your remembrance all things that I said to you."

If we are truly one in Messiah, we are not products of uniformity, we are like the fingerprint, each one possessing our own unique design. Therefore, let us teach New Testament discipline, through the leadership of the Holy Spirit, while encouraging personal relationship with Heavenly Father through divine intervention.

THE LOVE OF A JEWISH MESSIAH

Romans 8:28 says, "God causes all things to work together for the good of those who love Him, those who are called according to His purpose." This is one of the most beautiful qualities of the Messiah's love. However, in the chaos of conflict, it is often difficult to see or acknowledge divine activity. It is natural to default to despair. But heightened emotions can eclipse the love of the Messiah.

In that heated state of dispute, we run the risk of abandoning the reality of God's sovereignty. Once we enter that state of mind, it becomes easy to trust in human effort rather than divine intervention. Being incarcerated places severe limitations on your physical freedom. I was at the mercy of the state of North Carolina.

However, as I look back on that time in my life, I now understand that there are two types of imprisonment. One is the physical subjugation of your body, and the second is the subjugation of your mind. Believe me when I tell you, there is no darker dungeon than an oppressed mind.

The Bible says, in reference to Jesus, "Who the Son sets free is free indeed." Man can physically imprison your body, but only you can imprison your mind. It was the love of a Jewish Messiah that extended the beauty of true liberty to me. The conditions of my circumstances, and the dangers they posed, demanded total mental engagement. Prison culture is a world of its own, and allowing your mind to dwell on the world outside of prison walls can be mentally tormenting. I could not have known that within the confines of that environment, I would come to know and enjoy true freedom.

Jesus of Nazareth was born into the world for one purpose only: to die for the sins of humanity so that we might be reconciled to God. This alone amplifies the depth of God's love for the world. Furthermore, Jesus' courage and obedience, His willingness to abandon His own will and embrace God's will for His life, demonstrate His love for God. His three-and-a-half-year ministry is the blueprint—the foundation we use to establish our own harmonious walk with God. From the very first time I began to truly meditate on what He has done for me; I have wanted to live a life that honors Him, just as He honored God.

I began to practice a Messiah-centered lifestyle in an environment designed to bring out the worst in men. Prison culture can easily reduce a man to his most primal instincts. It perverts the sexuality of weak men. It is a culture of desperate men, and desperate men are unpredictable—men who, without warning, can become ruthless.

My greatest desire was to study the life of the Messiah. My greatest fear was that prison culture would cultivate the worst in me. Many times, I silently fought to keep the beast within me suppressed. On the few occasions when I was unsuccessful, I learned the beauty and power of repenting before those who were observing my struggle to follow a Jewish Messiah.

As I reflect on those years, I now see and understand the power of the Messiah's love—how it first impacts you and then convicts you to share it with your neighbor, i.e., the world. I cannot pinpoint exactly when it happened, but at some point, amid that prison culture, it became very important to me that the men around me saw Jesus within me.

My heart was responding to His love for me. Or, should I say, He had performed what the Bible calls a heart circumcision within me. He had taken my stony heart and replaced it with a tender heart of flesh—a heart that now pumped His life-giving blood to every fiber of my being, to the degree that even the vilest persons around me were now being affected.

My ambitious pursuit of the Messiah quickly became normal to me. The changes in me were subtle—so much so that I would only notice them when someone who knew me on the streets pointed out how different I was. I became totally infatuated with Jesus' love for me. Every free moment I had was dedicated to reading the Bible and memorizing Scripture. I was so caught up in the moments that I didn't even recognize—or, in most cases, realize—that the supernatural hand of God was consistently intervening on my behalf. Even in my failures, God was with me.

About a year and a half after I had been released from prison, I ran into a friend of mine whom I went to school with. Our paths had crossed again while in Raleigh, North Carolina's maximum-security prison. Eddie Jackson was in the population, and I was in processing, which meant I only had yard privileges once a week.

There were 600 men being housed in that prison, so the odds of the two of us having a brief reunion in the yard were highly unlikely. We reminisced for a few moments. That was my first and last time seeing him in prison. Standing in the parking lot of a convenience store, sharing stories about our prison experiences and naming friends who had died,

Eddie began to tell me about a plot to kill me while I was at the Raleigh prison.

Two men with whom I had violent encounters in my past life had made plans to avenge themselves—one of them completely against prison code. Unaware of our friendship, he revealed their plot to Eddie. Eddie told one of the officers. The next morning, I was shackled and placed on a prison van headed to another compound.

In their haste to get me out of harm's way, my paperwork got mixed up. As a result, once I finished processing, I was sent to a prison that eventually put me in a position to be transferred to a minimum-security prison after serving only a year. I was supposed to have been shipped to a maximum-security camp called Caledonia, which was said to be the worst prison camp in North Carolina.

I remember the day I got off the bus in Shelby, North Carolina. Within minutes of having my shackles removed, I found myself in the programmer's office being asked, "What are you doing on this camp?" "I have no idea, sir," was my response. I was told that, based on how my paperwork was written, they would have to allow me to go to school, which would delay my transfer to Caledonia by a year.

This was not bad news for me. I was less than a half-hour away from my family. I was also informed that it would be two weeks before a bunk in one of the dorms would be available, so I would have to sleep in solitary confinement for that time. This turned out to be a huge blessing. Although I had regular yard privileges, I only came out for meals.

While in processing, I had found a paperback Bible that someone had left behind—one of those "read the Bible in one year" books from PTL. The format was to read a chapter of the Old Testament in the morning, a Psalm, Proverb, or Ecclesiastes through Song of Solomon at noon, and a New Testament passage in the evening.

Within those two weeks of confinement, I read the entire Bible. I would take all my clothes off and read the Bible all day long. The officers always gave me the oddest looks when they walked past my cell, but I simply ignored them. I remember feeling as if the book was an extension of my body. Before the year had expired, I had read the Bible twice and was halfway through my third reading when the Holy Spirit prompted me to start studying it.

As I stood there in that parking lot, listening to Eddie and hearing for the first time how the hand of

God had moved on my behalf, I was amazed. God had directed each one of my steps, even placing me in solitary confinement for two weeks. Eddie must have thought I had lost my mind when I began to wipe tears from my eyes and loudly praise God.

Within the four years I spent in prison, I only had three violent outbursts. In the heat of those moments, and for some time afterward, I couldn't see how God had protected me and even used me to bring glory to Himself. Three violent outbursts—and all three men were twice my size. As someone charged with a violent crime, the last thing you want is to commit acts of violence while incarcerated.

Kenny Jolly was the first one to provoke me to anger. He was huge, a man in his mid-40s. Although concealed by fat, it was obvious that his body had once been sculpted. Still, Jolly was one of the strongest men on the weight pile. It was a hot summer day. The weight pile was filled with shirtless men pumping iron, laughing, egging each other on, grunting, and filling the air with obscenities.

At that point, I was still very small and had just started working out. I was unfamiliar with my way around the weight pile. I can't recall exactly what I did to provoke Jolly, but I remember him in my face, hurling profanities at me like a roaring lion. I stood there, silent. I was not afraid. I had mentally defaulted to my old nature. With my peripheral vision, I began to survey my surroundings to determine what I would use as a weapon to defend myself.

The silence was deafening. I could feel every eye on the weight pile fixed on me, waiting to see how I would respond. This moment would determine the level of respect I would get on that prison yard. Because of my small frame, it had taken me years to earn my reputation on the streets—a reputation that had kept me safe. I stood there, calculating in my mind: Was I prepared to sacrifice my reputation as a ruthless fighter for the sake of the reputation of this Jewish Messiah?

To add insult to injury, after Jolly had finished verbally abusing me, he casually laid down on the weight bench and proceeded to push 300 pounds off his chest. I stood there, my hands in front of me in a cuffed position, my teeth grinding. I could feel violence rumbling inside me like a volcano, and I felt as if I was incapable of stopping it from erupting. A vision flashed in my mind of hitting him in the throat, letting the weight fall on his chest, rendering him at my mercy.

Before I knew what was happening, I looked down at my perpetrator and calmly said, "This is your lucky day, Jolly." I then proceeded to exit the weight pile. All manner of tormenting thoughts filled my head as I made my way back to the dorm room. Jolly never apologized to me, but that was the last time he disrespected me. Oddly enough, my reputation as a genuine Christian skyrocketed on the yard. I found myself, for the first time, discipling other men. What the devil meant for evil, God used for good.

In 2 Corinthians 5:14, Paul writes, "The love of Messiah controls us." I did not realize it while I was in prison, but that's exactly what was happening. It was the love of Messiah that arrested me on that weight pile and provoked me to have mercy and speak a blessing over a man who had just heaped curses and insults on me.

My second violent outburst happened about eight months later, on that same prison yard. His name was Frank Hightower. He was a big and intimidating presence. It was rumored that Hightower had connections with the Aryan Brotherhood. Although none of his tattoos suggested any affiliation, he never confirmed or dispelled the rumors.

Hightower was mean. He had no problem hurling insults at anyone—Black, White, or Hispanic. He seemed to hate everyone. He was so intimidating that he frequently used the N-word when talking to Black men and was never challenged.

The school started four weeks after I arrived at that prison. By then, I had become comfortable with my surroundings. I had mentally sized up the 200-plus faces there and determined the level of threat they posed. As a product of the inner city, you look for motive when making eye contact. You assess strengths and weaknesses when interacting, and interacting was limited to men you knew on the streets or those assigned to the same dorm.

The only class that had an available slot for me was the electrical wiring class. I hated it. I absolutely dreaded going to that class every day. The thought of getting electrocuted fiercely intimidated me. But, as if that wasn't enough, Hightower was also in that class. It seemed as if every other day, Hightower found some way to verbalize his disdain for jailhouse religion.

My evangelistic zeal only served to agitate him even more. I did find it odd that he never directly addressed me with his insults toward Christianity, but that all changed when Hightower and I were put on the same team for the end-of-year project. The end-of-year project served as the final exam. Each team consisted of four men. My team included the best student in the class, Hightower, and I was the worst. The moment Hightower heard my name associated with his team, he began to object loudly, filling the room with profanity.

The entire class erupted in laughter. I can't remember our professor's name, but I can still see his constant gentle smile. Displaying that smile, he calmly asked the class to settle down, and as always, every man responded quickly. The assignment was to wire a wood-framed room, complete with electrical outlets, electrical switches, and a ceiling light. I broke out into a cold sweat just listening to the professor explain the assignment. He ended with, "You have two hours to complete the exam." He then turned and quickly sat down. Within that moment, everyone quickly began to gather their materials and choose a frame.

For the first time in those eight months, all of Hightower's insults were directly addressed to me. He used extremely offensive language to point out my dark complexion. Repeatedly, he labeled my obvious fear of electricity as stupidity. About 30 minutes into the project, Hightower's insults were having a noticeable effect—not just on me, but on the two other team members as well.

As Hightower's harassment intensified, I frequently glanced over at the professor, who was sitting calmly at his desk, preoccupied with reading an electrical wiring magazine. Periodically, I would catch the professor peering up from his magazine; he seemed somewhat amused by Hightower's behavior. This agitated me more than Hightower's insults.

With less than 45 minutes left to complete the assignment, my aggression erupted. I quickly unfastened my tool belt, and it dropped to the floor with a loud thump. The entire class came to a screeching halt. Until that moment, everyone had addressed me as "Rev," a common prison term for a Bible thumper. Now, without warning, I had totally regressed.

My voice deep and amplified, I roared profanities at Hightower. It was as if I was matching every racist remark he had made about Black people with my own hyper-negative opinions about White people. I stood far enough away from him to monitor his posture and be able to counteract his response. The professor stood up but said nothing. His smile was now replaced by a look of surprise and confusion. Hightower was noticeably stunned. He looked as if he was trying to mentally unpack what was happening before his eyes. His face was beginning to turn red. If he had wanted to respond, I didn't give him the opportunity. "When that lunch bell rings, you bring your #%&* down to the blind spot, and I'm gonna show you just how *#%& stupid I am," I said.

The blind spot was the side of the recreation building, hidden from the gun towers, where men would meet to settle disputes, among other unlawful things they wanted to conceal from the officers.

I could feel my face contorted with rage. Without taking my eyes off Hightower, I stepped out of the wooden frame and made my way over to the large window, gazing out over the yard. I kept Hightower in my peripheral vision and saw his surprise melt into anger. "It's on now," he said, ending his reply with the N-word.

The classroom was now filled with whispers as everyone slowly resumed working on their projects. As Hightower turned his attention back to wiring the wood frame, he added, "Your black #%*! belongs to me now, boy!"

I was out of the classroom door and making my way to the blind spot before the break bell finished ringing. Rage had consumed me, thrusting me forward. If the Holy Spirit was speaking to me, I was totally ignoring Him. As always, once the beast within me emerged, the adrenaline rushing through my body catapulted me into survival mode.

I knew I didn't stand a chance against Hightower. I didn't care—I would strike first and hard. Hightower would have to beat every ounce of fight out of me. I was so angry that I hadn't noticed the small crowd that had gathered by the time I reached the blind spot. The rage within me was so loud that it drowned out the conversations taking place around me.

I remember looking around, catching glimpses of the faces of men I had witnessed to. Those faces gave way to the lovingly convicting voice of the Holy Spirit, gently reminding me of what was at stake. I cannot describe the intensity of the internal conflict warring within my soul.

I wanted to yield to the voice of God; I wanted to abandon this violent course of action. Yet, at the same time, the thought of facing Hightower down promised such satisfaction. I remembered what it felt like to have street respect. I could not resist the desire to wear that cloak once again. Hightower pushed his way through the small crowd, stopping less than ten feet in front of me.

He just stood there, his hands at his sides, staring at me. His face looked different—almost as if he was at peace. I was too angry to be perplexed. I threw my fists up in front of my face, preparing to react to his assault. The spectators started to egg us on. They had come to witness a fight, and it was clear they didn't want to be disappointed.

It didn't take long for me to realize Hightower hadn't come to fight. Dropping my guard, I walked past him and pushed my way through the human circle that had formed. I walked melancholically back up the hill toward the dorm rooms. By then, guilt and shame had begun to harass me. I didn't return to class that day.

Instead, I went to my assigned dorm, climbed onto my bunk, and lay down. Staring at the ceiling, I felt tears slowly roll down the sides of my face and into my ears. Whether I was talking out loud or internally, I don't remember—I just began to ask God for forgiveness, repeatedly.

The next morning, I walked into that classroom, visibly humiliated. I stood in front of our professor and the 21 men in that classroom and asked them all to forgive me for my behavior. No one said a word. I moved to my desk and sat down. Being as unassuming as I could, I kept my eye on Hightower. He seemed to be ignoring me. I spent the remainder of my time on that camp anticipating the moment when Hightower would exact his revenge. It would be a year and a half later before I found out what God had done that day.

The favor of God was all over my life. Within a span of 18 months and two prison camps later, I was at Camp Green Minimum Custody Prison in Charlotte, North Carolina, my native city. I was on work release, enjoying home passes every other week. I had earned the respect of almost every inmate on the yard, but more than that, I had earned the respect of every officer on the camp.

I was seen by everyone there as a humble and godly person. God's incredible love had done a beautiful work in me and through me. I wanted everyone I encountered to experience that same overwhelming love. I had become a student of the Bible, memorizing a new scripture every week. But it was Galatians 5:5-6 that really influenced me. Those two passages remind us that love is the fuel of faith. Without genuine agape love—the charitable, unconditional love of God—you cannot operate in complete faith in God.

I had, at that point, been walking with God for a little over three years. The more I learned about God, the more I discovered about myself. And the more I discovered about myself, the more I realized just how desperately I needed God. I've found it is impossible to truly know the unmerited love of God until you have come face to face with your own depravity. The love of God filled my heart to such a degree that it compelled me to share my faith with everyone who would listen.

This resulted in many men accepting Jesus as their Messiah. I was a full-blown prison yard evangelist—a prison missionary. Armed only with the beautiful love of Messiah, I boldly shared His message of hope, and it consistently penetrated even the hardest of hearts. It was a Wednesday evening. I got off the work release bus, walked through the gate, was searched for contraband, and signed in.

Before I could make my way to the dorm room, two young men that I was discipling ran up to me. With fear on their faces, they whispered simultaneously, as if everyone was listening, "Hightower got off the transfer bus today; he's on the yard." I'm certain they could not read my reaction. They could not detect the mild anxiety that was rising within me. My survival mode has always chosen to fight rather than flee. I had concluded at a very early age that a display of fear was a man's greatest weakness.

I had taken my shower, dressed, and proceeded to the recreation building to set it up for Yoke Fellowship. This was what we called our Wednesday night Bible study. A group of volunteers, men and women, would come in and sit at tables that typically consisted of two volunteers and four residents. Each table would discuss whatever that evening's Bible topic was.

A moment of silence came over me as I looked up toward the door to see Hightower walk in and take a seat at one of the tables. Neither I nor Hightower spoke to each other that evening. The next evening, I sat at a table on the yard, talking to three of the gentlemen that I was discipling. I remember vividly talking to them about Jesus being the truth, the way, and the life.

I continued talking as Hightower came into focus. He was about 50 yards away from me, his gaze fixed on me as he began to make his way toward me. I stopped talking, my eyes fixed on him as I waited for the confrontation. Hightower stopped and stood on the other side of the table where I was sitting.

"What's up, Rev?" was his salutation.
"Not much, what's up with you, Hightower?" I replied.

The next words that came out of his mouth stunned me. "Jesus is what's up, man! I gave my life to Jesus last year," Hightower exclaimed as he quickly sat down and began to share his testimony. That was a beautiful day.

Hightower soon became one of my disciples. One day, as he and I walked the yard together, I asked him, "Brother, do you remember when we almost came to blows at the Shelby Camp?" "Yeah, yeah, I remember, man. That was a weird day, brother. I was walking down the hill thinking about how I was going to tear you apart.

All of a sudden, I hear this voice saying, 'If you don't put your guard up, he won't hit you.' Right after that, I started feeling scared. When I got to the blind spot, standing in front of you, it was like my hands were being pressed to my sides. I couldn't say a word. Bro, I'm telling you, I've never been that scared in my life. The next morning, when you came into the classroom and asked everybody to forgive you, man, this peace came over me, and it's never left me to this day."

As I listened to Hightower, the love of Messiah began to flood my heart. God's love not only protected me that day but also ministered to Hightower, giving him the one thing he needed more than anything else—the peace of God. The love of this Jewish Messiah is so far-reaching; it wants to touch the heart of every soul on the planet. What He's done in me, what He did in Hightower, and what He's done in so many of those I have led to Messiah is powerful, beautiful, and life-changing. That's the love of this Jewish Messiah.

THE COMPOSITION OF
A BLACK MAN

To be an inner-city Black man in America is to be a man of desperation. When the surveying of your environment confirms your sense of hopelessness, it can reduce your ambitions to mere pipe dreams. The nature of a man is to provide for and protect his family. The inner city, however, begins to pervert the natural instinct of a man from the first day of his introduction to its chaos.

Fatherless homes, minimum wage jobs, extremely burdened mothers, streets infested with brutal criminal elements, despairing beggars, self-medicating zombies, pain, death and lots of death were all the inner-city seemed to offer its people. The inner-city Black man finds himself defining free enterprise as a drug pusher, thievery and, or robbery. The mentality is one or the other, be hustled, or be the hustler. The message is dog eat dog.

Darwin's theory of organisms states, "the best adjusted to their environment, are the most successful." To those seemingly condemned to this American nightmare, Darwin's theory is taken to an entirely new level. It feels as if even God stays clear of the violent streets of the inner city. Where does this leave a Black man-child?

Children are born with an intrinsic desire to be fathered. It takes one generation of fatherlessness to grossly pervert a boy's God given desire to be fathered. Place that scenario within the confines of a people contained in impoverished conditions. The average American cannot even begin to fathom the horrendously negative impact a boy, Black or White, emerging from such an environment, will have on his community.

Given my upbringing in the inner city, my childhood was short lived. It seems as if overnight I transitioned from baby formula to malt liquor, chewing bubble gum to smoking weed, from bicycles to stolen vehicles, from cardboard clubhouses to drug infested liquor houses. Somewhere between the madness, I lost my virginity. By the time I started junior high school I had earned a reputation for being fearless and cold hearted.

My younger siblings and I enjoyed the ambiance of safety that my reputation afforded us. Within the culture that produced me, a boy determines his own age of Bar Mitzvah. Where there is no clear depiction of fathering, determined manhood comes down to a boy's own assessment of self, coupled with the intensity of his struggle to survive and desire to thrive. I had no concept of the power of fatherly counsel. My mother did the best that she could in trying to be both a mother and a father to me. However, a woman is very limited in her ability to help a boy transition into manhood.

As a ten-year-old boy, who had never visited a church, I remember as a child thinking it was strange that 98 percent of the homes had, for some reason, embraced a long, blonde haired, bearded, blue-eyed, White man. I had no idea who this Yeshua was and every house I went into seemed to have mounted on their wall, at least one of the two pictures I had ever seen of him.

One picture was a head and shoulders shot of Yeshua looking peacefully into the heavens, the other was of him standing before a huge arched top wooden door, knocking. These two pictures were very popular in the late 60's and early 70's.

I was an uninformed Black child, living in an era where children were to be seen, compliant, and silent. I concluded this Yeshua to be out of place. I admit, despite the picture's misrepresentation of Messiah, something deep within my childish mind reverenced it.

I am attempting to evaluate those faint moments of emotional reverence I experienced as a child. A young Black boy raised in that era of time, being intimidated by the adult world, remembered gazing at only the two portraits of Yeshua available. I did not dare ask why this White man hung on our wall.

Now, looking back from the perspective of a believer, I am even more convinced of man's intrinsic need to acknowledge the unseen force of divinity.

I now realize, whether a man chooses to embrace or reject what his heart knows to be true, this is a decision that he must consistently struggle with in life. Over the course of time, everyone must validate divinity or cynically deny it. Man will instinctually move towards a deeper spirituality. The acknowledgement or rejection of divinity is always the result of an encounter.

I was thirty years old when I surrendered my life to the God of glory. Initially I found it very difficult to wrap my mind around the concept of God being a loving father to me. Not only was my concept of fathering grossly perverted, I also harbored an underlying disdain for male authority figures.

By far, my greatest challenge was embracing a Savior whom at the time, I thought was White. I was oblivious to the fact that Yeshua was Jewish. However, from my reality, whether Jewish, European or Indian, regarding the consequence of nationality, the world was anti-Black. In my mind, not being born a Black man-child in the projects was the one thing Yeshua could celebrate.

A PEOPLE OF INTENSITY

I have always viewed Black people as a people of intense passion from my childhood as far back as I can remember. Amid my mother and siblings as well as other relatives, the immense passion of the Black experience has captivated me. I lived in many different neighborhoods and attended various schools. I made friends and foes through it all, including the workforce. However, the one thing that remains consistent is the depth of the passion in Black people.

My views were formed from the perspective of my entire childhood being a world of predominantly light and dark-complexioned Black people. As a youth, relationships with people who looked like me and shared the same social scale influenced my worldview. These people shaped both my expectations and aspirations for my future.

I understand now that my world back then and now only represented a small percentage of Black America. Therefore, I have drawn my conclusions from an assessment of the historical Black experience in America including my own experience as a Black American, and finally, from some speculation.

The Black Americans' deep and soulful passions are expressed through our foods, our attire, our walk, our body language, and even the way we talk. The presence of the Black man displays a creativity that has fascinated on-looking ethnic groups for centuries. The Black American people are a beautiful and graceful race.

Compassionate by nature, our emotions drive our hearts and our intensity can easily be mistaken for anger. We are survivors, tested and proven. We have endured bondage, genocide, and extreme racism, even the loss of our identity. For centuries in America, and in some cases even we ourselves have viewed our Blackness as a curse rather than a blessing. Could this be why we so readily embraced the Caucasian Yeshua?

The nappy hair, big noses and broad lips, are all synonymous with Blackness. However, promoting the embracing of our distinctness for its beauty have been mere windows in time. Catchy phrases such as, "Say it loud, I'm Black and I'm proud," coined by James Brown, the afro, addressing each other as soul brothers and sisters, and even the Black man referring to his woman as his Black Queen all seemed to open Black America's eyes for a moment.

However, bridging the gap between lighter and darker skinned Blacks, as well as the economic classes, has been an exhausting effort. In spite of valiant attempts to unify ourselves, we have yet to find common ground by which to stand in one accord.

This has always been a point of deep crisis for Blacks. Historically speaking, the Black American's spirituality has always been a source of great strength for him. Unfortunately, even our spirituality has failed to unite us soulfully. Black Americans' view of Yeshua, even genuine Christianity, has become so distorted that it now fails to offer true spiritual guidance.

Like White America, when our spiritual caregivers are overly educated, they become indoctrinated into secularism. The poorly educated gradually become intoxicated with the unmerited reverence so enthusiastically offered to them by parishioners.

Both eventually superimpose rigid commands on those seeking spiritual enlightenment. Commands far removed from God's original intent. From its inception, the Black church has offered honor and prestige to those who in most cases have not earned it, and thereby misused and abused the honor. The Black church has desired gifted entertainers and given them superstar status. In exchange, she (the church) has received an ineffective gospel message. The message has passively abandoned its efforts to touch, change, and draw the hearts of the hearers into a deeper relationship with God through Messiah.

The gifted entertainer has packaged and presented a message that has the look and the feel of something beautiful as well as powerful. However, in reality the message of the gospel has gone from being plausible to comical. For this debacle, the Black church has only herself to blame. When we elevate men, we sacrifice the genuine presence of God and His anointing.

I believe we have always been a people at the very brink of tapping into our deep and rich spirituality. Like many other ethnic groups and cultures, in our failure to interpret supreme truth correctly, we have reduced Christianity to a wall of prohibitions. It has become a list of do's and don'ts that serve only to disfigure the beauty of the gospel and keep us from entering into God's glory.

Although I did not come from a spiritual home, I was briefly exposed to the rich, but awkward, spirituality of my people at an early age. I was ten years old when I had my first encounter with church. I remember vividly a host of crazy emotions: fear, dismay, and utter confusion.

It was a backyard revival held behind one of the apartments in the government-housing complex that we lived in at the time. The preacher was a small man with one dead eye, a big Afro, and porkchop (wide) sideburns. I remember roaming through our neighborhood long after my seven o'clock curfew. It was a warm mid-July night, my adventurous friends and I curiously stumbled upon an emotionally charged gathering. I remember it being dark. The only light came from a few porch lights and the bright full moon that seemed to be shining down on this backyard revival.

The preacher wore a beautiful black robe as he, like a ball of intense rage, spit out a fire and brimstone sermon. The intense expression of what appeared to be anger on his face held me captive. As I gave studious attention to the rage behind the blazing words, I saw on his face what appeared to be a small but warm smile. It drew me in, yet at the same time, confused me. How could this man be so angry, yet so comforting?

My focus began to shift from the face of this fiery preacher, to the faces of the seemingly out of control congregation. My confusion only intensified as a mixture of whaling cries and shouts of, "Amen, thank you Yeshua and Hallelujahs," filled the night air. I remember people passing out, fierce body jerking, and rapid gibberish chanting. The whole scene would have been comical had I not been so overcome with fear. There I was at the tender age of ten amid utter chaos, all done in the name of Yeshua. This simply added to my confusion. I knew nothing about the name Yeshua at that moment.

It was out of that childhood experience that I learned to equate the name of Yeshua with the paranormal. Less than a year later, I would have a terrifying encounter with that preacher. It scared my conscious and left a bitter taste in my mouth concerning Christianity.

I had started attending that fiery preacher's church on Friday evenings via an old school bus cheaply converted into a church bus. Having marked out the words school bus on its sides, the back door and the top front with black spray paint, this bright orange bus would pick up a group of us from my neighborhood and take us to a small storefront church. Although my mother never went, she did not have a problem with me attending with a few of my friends. One evening I had been picking on some girls, joking around with them. In an attempt to get back at me they told the preacher they had seen me searching his coat pockets as it hung on a coat rack beside the bench I was sitting on that night.

As I sat on the bench talking with two other boys while waiting for the bus to come for us, suddenly, as if he came out of nowhere, with great force this preacher jerked me up by my shoulders and violently screamed, "What were you doing in my coat pockets!" Tiny drops of his saliva projected from his mouth and splattered onto my quivering face. With his arms extended gripping my small frame, I stood paralyzed between the firm grips of his hands. I could feel his boney fingers digging into the ball-joints of my shoulders. I replied nervously and hesitantly, "I was not in your coat pockets."

With piercing eyes, he angrily persisted, "I can look into your eyes and tell you're lying," he said as if he despised me. He reduced me to a mass of humiliation, I cried uncontrollably. I have no remembrance of the bus ride home or anything else equated to that event. Even today, the stark memory of that event, is as if it was an isolated moment in time. Where could I go to find solace and safety? I was born in 1962, signifying I grew up in an age amid the beauty and freedom of the early 1970's where afros, Black exploitation movies, plaid suits, bell-bottom pants as well as Disco music was all a part of that era.

My cultural concepts of my Blackness and identity as a Black man were cultivated amid the inner-city with adult struggles that included poverty, alcoholism, drug abuse and sexual promiscuity. I spent my time practically on every Saturday of my most impressionable young teen years in a dark movie house glorifying seemingly larger than life Black men and women that were unable to maintain healthy relationships. These super-violent pimps, pushers and womanizers became my preachers and teachers.

The theater became my church as I sat among a congregation hurling profanity that communicated amen to the immorality displayed by our dismal heroes. Unrecognizable at the time during this process, my world became as dark as the movie theater I sat in going through a spiritual experience as a young teenager. Years would pass before I would come to terms with the effects those images and ideologies would ultimately have on my spirituality. My sense of self became as distorted as the characters that influenced my childish mind. Internally, I began a descent into darkness, spiraling down a road of self-destruction fueled by drugs and alcohol. I was totally out of touch with my spirit man. A man I had no idea even existed.

I have defined the Black American as highly emotional and a people of great intensity. Everything about the Black race, and the Black man particularly, expresses a soulful mystery, possessing an inner strength so grand that at times he himself has found it difficult to harness.

His incredible God given gifts, his distinctive sounds (vocal and instrumental), his physical features (unbelievable coordination and beautiful pigmentation), and his wonderful creativity (sense of self-expression) has been feared, envied, appreciated as well as often emulated.

However, it is the Black man's spirituality, his relationship with Yeshua Messiah, the Jewish man praised by Christianity as God and Savior, that still remains the most mysterious spiritual aspect of the Black man's makeup. It is a mystery even unto himself; a relationship riddled with unanswered questions. Why would the Black man embrace a religion that brutally brought him bound in shackles into a strange land and delivered him into the hands of so-called Christians? Those same Christians who would use their religion in an attempt to establish supremacy over him.

Why would he embrace a Messiah, rejected by his own people? Moreover, why would a Black man blessed with such inner strength feel the need for a crutch? These are questions that demand answers only by those that stand outside of the body of Yeshua and have no desire to understand genuine Christianity.

There are, however, several pressing questions I feel are legitimate and worthy of addressing. What is the origin of the seemingly chaotic church meetings, and do they serve any real purpose? Above all, is the Black man's relationship with Messiah one that was forced on him by White America or is it God ordained? To not answer the latter question first, in my opinion would be a case of putting the cart before the horse.

BLACKS AND JEWS:
A SHARED HISTORY

I believe it is necessary to address the question of the origin of the Black man's relationship with Messiah from both a secular and ecclesiastical perspective. Moses was married to an Ethiopian woman (Numbers 12:1). It was an Ethiopian man that saved the life of the prophet Jeremiah (Jeremiah 13:7-13). God personally sent Philip to tell a high-ranking Ethiopian eunuch about Yeshua (Acts 8:25-39).

In the book of Acts 13:1 we read of a prophet and teacher named Simeon who was called Niger, which translates, Black man. Secularly speaking, should we consider it coincidental that Blacks and Jews have been repeatedly and viciously targeted for genocide? In addition, these two ethnic groups have been belittled, hated, persecuted and misunderstood on a global level throughout the historical records of time.

I suspect spiritual conspiracy at the hands of principalities who are extremely hostile towards God's agenda. I understand the dark forces of hostility towards the Jewish community. They are God's chosen people and a very intricate part of God's plan of soul harvesting during the tribulation period. However, I do not see the reasoning behind the excessive energy that has gone into the calculated demise of the Black man. Could it be that the wicked spiritual beings that hover between the third heavens and the earth are fearful of a God plan that involves the Black man? That is a concept, not a revelation.

We know that three major religions, Judaism, Islam, and Christianity, came out of the Middle East. These three religions were birthed out of one man, Abraham. Furthermore, these three religions are the most recognized in all the world. No other religions have come close to the influence these three have in all the world.

It is a fact that hundreds of years before the slave trade, that these three religions spread like wildfire throughout the Middle East. Therefore, the logical assumption is that the slave ships, which departed from those coasts bound for Europe and America, housed Christians and Muslims.

With that being said, it is highly unlikely any of these African captives practiced Judaism. Given the depth and extremities of the spiritual commitment found in the Middle East, it is a reasonable conclusion that those who lived for a certain religion would be prepared to die for it as well. I would even go as far as saying that the believers who emerged from the putrid bellies of those slave ships, narrowly escaping death, not only survived because of their faith, but also developed a deeper dependency on this Jewish Messiah.

It is a fact that genuinely religious people who experience extreme trauma will deepen their convictions concerning their faith. It is humanly impossible for any individual to survive unscathed after being subjected to callous mental and physical trauma. Though their outer appearance may appear to be strong and injury free, even they themselves find it difficult to pinpoint the inner damage that has accrued in their mind, soul, and spirit.

Some people develop extremely aggressive person- alities due to prolonged trauma exposure while others may become overly passive. These personality deviations from the norm are defense mechanisms. The symptoms range from social detachment, reck- lessness, poor impulse control, self-hatred, destruc- tive, and manipulative behavioral patterns to name a few.

Our society deals with these social disorders either by some sort of isolation, therapy, and or drugs (legal and illegal).

Believers, on the other hand, upon entering into a traumatizing experience, not only believe God is with them, but that by keeping their focus on God trust that He will work in them as well as through them to bring about a positive change within themselves along with all those they encounter. The believer truly believes his Messiah is with him straightening and strengthening him from within his inner man. The believer determines in his suffering that he will bring glory to his God.

I have found that the genuine Christian will come out of the traumatizing experience bearing the scars, yet confident in his and her expectations of a better tomorrow.

Their demeanor may bear the reluctance of one twice burned, yet their eyes display a subdued steady stream of light that communicates, "I see the approaching beauty that Messiah promised, not even death can preclude it." Their actions, while disturbingly gentle, boldly proclaim, "God loves you." The genuine follower of this Jewish Messiah is a wonderfully beautiful expression of the person of God on the earth.

Christians view their sufferings as being insignificant in comparison to the sufferings of this

Yeshua. I view the person with this type of mindset as being the possessor of an unconquerable spirit. His defiance, though restrained, is visible so much so that his oppressors struggle to resist their own feelings of intimidation by his inner courage.

Throughout history, in an effort to bring his body and mind under the oppressor's control, the unconquerable spirit has been met with extreme acts of violence. The intimidated are always the most violent. Even still, the authentic integrity of those whose inner passion is the pursuit of Yeshua-likeness is an uncomfortable offense to anyone whose lifestyle defies sacred scripture. It is also an equally uncomfortable conviction to anyone whose desires are stimulated by conscious.

I believe the inner strength and integrity of the Black man was responsible for the inhumane brutalities he suffered at the hands of his White brothers, as was the freedom he ultimately received by that same hand. Responsible, but not to blame, was that same inner strength and integrity within the person of Yeshua, which prompted the Jewish leaders to respond to him violently. It also fueled the Holocaust. The list goes on and on; however, the end is consistently the same. When the smoke finally clears, the unconquerable spirit is still standing.

I am not attempting to make or suggest Christianity the only source capable of producing the unconquerable spirit. However, I do want to make two clear distinctions; no other religion offered such hope, and no other religion had such a visible and positive impact on the enslaved Black man.

I certainly believe there were African Christians taken from their native land, enslaved, violently abused, and morally degraded. Nevertheless, it was a grossly perverted Christianity or biblical message superimposed on the African captives designed to promote White supremacy, which ultimately empowered the Black man with the hope he would need to survive the brutal voice roaring, "This is your fate and it is sealed." I find the irony of it all bittersweet. The gospel message and its power to liberate the mind are so profound that any attempt to pervert it, regardless of its shrewdness, will ultimately fail. This is a historical given.

The enslaved African was told he was created inferior to his White counterparts. That his dark skin was a mark of shame placed on him by God because of the sin of Cain. The African was told that his service to the White race was God ordained. But the message of this Jewish man, with his claims of deity, of Sonship with God, of God's intense love not just for a race, but for all of humanity finds its way into the desperate hearts of those who long for truth. It takes root, and sobering hope overshadows stormy desperation. The message of this Jewish Messiah gives an inner peace which enables His followers to anticipate the pending sunrise while enduring the blackest night of their souls.

It is a message of genuine love, courage and unimaginable loyalty. It bridges the gap between man and his maker and gives meaning to his existence and beauty to his eternity. It then further compels him to embrace the energy God has placed within him.

For the enslaved Christians, emancipation came long before President Lincoln. Lincoln would deliver physical freedom to the enslaved Africans, yet, Messiah would free their minds. Better still, Messiah kept their minds free. This Jewish Messiah inspired the powerful Negro spirituals, the fiery hope in Yeshua centered sermons that would become synonymous with the Black Church.

The German Theologian, Dietrich Bonhoeffer, while in New York attending the Union Theological Seminary, was deeply impacted after being exposed to the depth of Black spirituality in a Harlem

Church. As a result, his sense of Christian duty would overshadow his every decision from that point on. Black Americans, desiring nothing more than equality, stood on the doctrine of Messiah and compelled a nation to feel the pain and sense of degradation that Blacks had to cope with daily.

It was Messiah's strength and courage shining through a people that gently demanded their recognition as first-class citizens. Blacks following His doctrine prompted White America to take a horrifying gaze at the atrocious acts of brutality and injustices they endured at the hands of a nation that hated them for no other reason than the color of their skin. Messiah's doctrine prompted the courage of non-violent protests, and created a people empowered to stand against unthinkable repercussions. This Jewish Messiah laid the groundwork for a gentle rebellion, and thereby brought the aggression of racism to its knees. Black Americans may never see Yeshua in that light, nevertheless He is creditworthy.

What are the possibilities of today's Black America experiencing the power of trusting in, and living out the commands of this great leader? Gone is the church filled with the chaos of desperation, a people driven to congregate by loss of family, manhood, and womanhood, fashioned into sources of encouragement, one to the other. Black America has followed the lead of his White brothers; we have fashioned a Messiah to which we can relate.

We have darkened his complexion, given him a bigger nose, fuller lips, and dreadlocks. We have mounted this image on our walls and called him Yeshua. The problem with this image is that like the earlier images I encountered as a boy, it moves you further away from the beauty, power, and mystery of the historical Yeshua. God incarnate, born into a specific race of people, lived among them as their Savior exclusively. Rejected and killed by them, rose from the dead to become the Savior of humanity exclusively.

Having weighed the evidence, I have drawn what I consider the only logical decision; I embrace this Jewish Messiah as my Lord and Savior. The fact that I am a Black man, in terms of the purpose of Yeshua Messiah, is of no relevance. The pigmentation of a man's skin, in relation to his pursuit of Messiah, holds no significance.

What a man brings to the body of Messiah, "the Church", by way of cultural dynamic, plays a critical role. Cultural clash provokes the Church, forcing her into a state of perpetual evolution. Therefore, it is passively, and, in some cases, blatantly resisted. The clashing of culture demands a breaking from tradition. It is the invasion of new ideas, the challenging, and sometimes, the condemning of old mindsets.

My assessment of this Jewish Messiah has been from the standpoint of an inner-city Black man. How has Yeshua affected my life? In the same way He has affected much of history. I am what I am because the light of truth prevailed in my life, in spite of the dark images that either moved me away from or projected hideous misrepresentation of the message and character of this Jewish Messiah.

My relationship with this Yeshua, the One that died and now lives, has deeply affected, and influenced me. There are times when my walk with him resembles a fierce struggle. I am a different man, a new man, yet, far too often my humanity is as dark as that movie theater that once served as my refuge.

My manhood, at times can be as fragile as that terrified child that quivered between the clutches of a crazed and insensitive preacher. Yet, it is this intrinsic fellowship with a divine interpreter, known to those born again as Holy Spirit that I find my equilibrium. Holy Spirit is the indwelling presence of God released into the earth by a resurrected Messiah. A Messiah that has ascended into the third heaven and now sits at the right hand of God.

According to the biblical instruction of Yeshua, His followers understand His doctrine as Holy Spirit brings it to their remembrance and interprets it. I draw courage and peace of mind from Holy Spirit. This third part of the Godhead has become a compass within my spirit man.

I was 30 years old when I surrendered my life and will over to God. I underwent the ceremony of baptism three years later while on a weekend home pass from a minimum-security prison. I publicly demonstrated what had taken place within me. The burial of the old man and the rising of the new; this took place in the warm muddy waters of a lake behind an old holiness church.

20 years after having been horrifyingly humiliated at the hands of a misguided preacher, that same Pastor would gently plunge me beneath the mucky waters of that, otherwise, beautiful lake. The pastor had no recollection of the boy, now a man. The same hands that once clutched my shoulders viciously tormenting me, now with one hand caressed the

back on my neck, while the other pressed my crossed hands to my chest. He would take part in one of the most memorable events in my life.

My grandmother had been a faithful member at the church for over 15 years. Virginia Brown had always been a woman of few words, stern in face and posture. This day, Virginia did not even attempt to mask the utter joy she was experiencing.

I stood before my grandmother amongst ten others all adorned in white robes and in our bare feet. The grandson Sister Brown had devoted thousands of hours in prayer for was now preparing to publicly validate his spiritual journey.

Many years would pass before I would come to understand, although the Church was a very vital component concerning my contribution to the body of Messiah, her role concerning the intimacy of my relationship with God was and is significantly small. I now realize the Church, "the gathering of the called-out ones", prepares me for spiritual warfare. Time alone with God prepares me for eternity. Intimacy establishes relationship. We achieve genuine discovery of self through our depth of relationship with the Creator.

God designed humanity with the capacity for interaction with the divine. Human spirituality accounts for fifty percent of our powers of engagement; it seeks to be one with God, self, and humankind. The intellect accounts for forty percent of our power to engage. It attempts oneness with the universe, self, and humankind, and our sensuality accounts for ten percent; its power to engage extends only to humankind. All three levels of engagement: spiritual, intellectual, and sensual are stimulated by selfish motives. Ironically, to attempt self-discovery through self-gratification is mere self-deception. Sadly enough, the one deceived is always the last to perceive.

In my pursuit of God, through His Jewish Son Yeshua, my true self was unveiled. The man that my environment had cultivated began to feel like an intruder. I wanted to put as much distance as I could between my former self and the man I perceived would be acceptable as a leader in mainstream Christendom. I now realize that deep within me I was pursuing the validation of White America.

I was ashamed of how I expressed myself. My occasional use of slang language and broken English, my preference of attire, even the emotional content of my preaching was offensive to me.

I sought God concerning this perceivable cultural handicap. God's response to me was consistently the same, "You are who you are; you are accepted in the beloved." I wish I could say those words brought comfort to me. The truth is, I took very little solace in Ephesians 1:11.

In the process of time, I would come to realize that although I was very thankful for the redemptive work of Yeshua the Messiah, I was not satisfied with it. In short, I was pursuing affirmation from a culture that found my desire to be embraced uncomfortable. I felt like a porcupine.

I would often cry out in frustration, "Oh my God! Your people, my brothers and sisters, are never going to see me as anything more than a redeemed convict." I saw myself in the eyes of the Church, as a mere special project from the other side of the tracks.

The gentle voice of Holy Spirit would consistently rehearse in my ear, "You are who you are; you are accepted in the beloved." The season would come when I was ready to receive what God had been communicating to me. In the same way I received redemption by God through His only begotten Son, I moved into deeper relationship with God through the same Son.

My calling is not to seek relationship with God through His body, the Church, but rather to bless His body by seeking relationship with Him, through Yeshua, the Messiah. My cultural molding had produced a unique man God had a plan and purpose for. The internal offense those in the body of Christ experienced by the hideousness of my past or the ineptness of my social strengths revealed their own spiritual weaknesses.

Regarding the believer, the establishing of spiritual strength is in his or her ability to fix their focus on a Jewish Messiah. Racial profile and cultural orientation serve only as highlighters which illuminate the beauty, mercy and majesty of our God.

I am a Black man following a Jewish Messiah, but I am part of a body called to do likewise. God, in His sovereignty gave me my black skin; He sanctioned the culture from which I came. Through His Son, this Jewish Messiah, I have been drastically changed.

Albeit, much of my own culture I now retain and understand that in the eyes of my God, this is a good thing. I will even go as far as to say that to the body of Messiah, "the Church", my blackness, my culture and even my relationship with Messiah is indeed the gift I bring. In the eyes of God, my past is not my testimony.

According to the Bible, because of the blood of Yeshua, God refuses to deposit my past into His memory bank. The moment I received His forgiveness, God removed my sin-filled history as far as the east is from the west, cast into the sea of forgetfulness.

One of Apostle Paul's signature statements for Christian productivity is, "Forgetting those things which are behind me." My testimony is constantly being established in my daily walk with my God as Holy Spirit leads me from victory to victory, from glory to glory, molding me more and more into Messiah-likeness. Paul's past was a repulsive scare, and at times he would have to explain it. However, his testimony, the Greek word used is *martyrias* (witness, evidence given, reputation, report), is how he lived out his everyday walk with Messiah.

PERSONAL ESTEEM

The definition of personal esteem is, to have a realistic respect for or favorable impression of one's self. I was seven months premature and very dark skinned, my name, Morris, translates; of dark complexion. My mother once told me as a newborn she could fit me in a shoebox. She shared how her friends would tease her, making statements such as, "Your baby looks like a hairless rat."

Consider this, I was born in an era when the most brutal acts of racist behavior were perpetrated by Blacks against Blacks, i.e. the lighter versus the darker complexioned Blacks. I credit and admire Nora Kay, my beautiful mother, for advertently doing her best to instill within me a sense of self-value that would empower me to cope with being very dark and poor in the inner city.

I unflinchingly faced a world that looked down on me, simply because of the color of my skin, because Nora instilled within me that my black complexion was beautiful. My mother's hugs, her enthusiastic voice, intentionally and lovingly calling me her black beauty prepared me for the ridicule my peers would one day hurl at me. I was mockingly called Tar-Baby, black spook, and smoky. Even adults would say things such as, "Boy, you so black til you blue." However, no mockery could penetrate the wall of security my mother had constructed around my heart. I was absolutely convinced my Blackness was beautiful.

By the time I got my first summer job, momma's repeated instruction to me rang inside my head, "Don't let the White man have to tell you to do something twice. You have to work twice as hard as a White man. Ain't nothing worse than a lazy Black man."

By the time my mother was 20 years old she was a widow, the mother of a one-year old son, and pregnant with my younger sister Sandra. I was a man before I ever heard my mother even mention the fear, uncertainty, and emotional stress she underwent. Looking back, my mother was constantly preparing me to face the world as a Black man. Her experiences undoubtedly shaped her worldview.

In 1960 my mother was a petite 16-year-old. One evening shortly after dusk, my mother and a group of her friends were standing on a corner, a favorite teen gathering place. The teens where innocently singing doo-wop, dancing, and enjoying each other when a car came racing by. A White man hanging out of the passenger side window furiously shouted over the sound of screeching tires, "Get your Black asses out of the street!" He flashed a gun and fired several shots into the unsuspecting group of teens. One of the bullets found my mother's hip. In a sweeping motion, a male friend responding to my mother's agonizing cry, snatched her up, with both arms he clinched her to his chest and began to run. Amid all of the panic and frantic scurrying, the young man, in a momentary loss of wit, burst through the door of a nearby corner store wide eyed and panting violently, holding my howling mother in his arms, his pants drenched in her blood.

In a desperate plea for help the young man cried out, "Help her! She's been shot!" At that very moment, the young man realized what he had just done. The store attendant looked up from behind the counter; two male customers turned and faced the two teenagers. The three men were white and clearly had no intentions of helping. The store attendant, with piercing cold eyes, snarled angrily. He began his demand with the "N" word, "If you don't get out of this store, I'm gonna shoot you!"

Obviously, the America which had shaped my mother's worldview is far different from today's America. My mother prepared me to face a White America based on her assessment. Not once did

Nora Kay encourage me to hate, she simply made it clear that White America viewed me as being inferior. I am almost certain that I, whether passive or otherwise, communicated that same sentiment to my own children. I am equally certain a very large percentage of White American homes communicated the same school of thought, whether passive or otherwise.

Historically, the issue of racial divide has been and continues to be one of great difficulty, to the degree that the greater society chooses the proverbial elephant in the room approach, the Church being without exemption. The Church is increasingly desegregating, but genuine unity continues to evade her. True unity is cultivated in the one-on-one relationship with God through Messiah.

Unity compels us to first seek to understand one another, and second, to seek to protect one another. If I do not truly know you, I cannot earnestly love you. We instinctively profile by color, but ethnic profiling has the potential to divide because of social dogmas and subconscious phobias.

Human nature fears what it does not understand. It is also human nature to attempt to subdue, control, or eradicate that which we perceive to be a threat to our illusion of security. Thus, the implementation of the most sophisticated form of human or ethnic annihilation– the divesting of self-esteem to provoke self-destruction.

It is impossible to extend respect, admiration, appreciation, and value toward another if it has not first been established within self. Based on the events that have influenced and shaped our individual worldviews, we will interpret and respond differently to the crises we see and hear unfolding before us.

True unity is not in uniformity but in our ability to cultivate a love and respect first, for the heart of our God, and then one another. The message of Messiah promotes personal esteem by declaring the depth of God's love for us. God turned His only begotten Son over to the hand of evil, that those that would look with confidence to Him would have their sin debt removed.

The sin debt has prompted humanity to devalue our own sense of self-worth. From God's inception of humanity, He declares a very high value of us, "Let us make man in our image." In Hebrews 2:6-7 the question is asked, "What is man, that you are mindful of him, you designed him just a little lower than the angelic beings and crowns him with glory and honor." If God Himself established the value of a human being, is it not sacrilege for those who believe on Him to de-value the worth of a man?

By reason of the shed blood of the Son of God, the issue of personal esteem is extremely elevated. In reference to the Church, "the Body of Christ," we are all members in particular, (one of the constituent parts of a whole).

To acknowledge Jesus as the Savior of the world, to accept him as your Messiah, is to embrace your God given destiny. Through a Jewish Messiah God extends new breath to the dormant spirit of those indisputably surrendered to His unremitting pursuit.

The revitalized spirit of a man has an obligation to strengthen the Church. God desires for His creation to behold His kingdom in operation. He wants to show forth His spectacular glory amid a world that has very little regard for Him.

If the world is to realize its great need for the grace and mercy of the Godhead, the church must become the unified body God intended her to be. More than anything else, the world needs to see a unified church– a body of believers who possess tremendous love one for another. Genuine, sacrificial, selfless love can agitate the foundations of religion and denominations.

The strength and attraction of religion and denominations is its primary doctrinal focus on improving, sustaining, and changing an individual's quality of life, aiding and abetting us in our relentless pursuit of happiness. Any doctrine that places the emphasis on human development will predominantly produce opinionated humanitarians, self-centered, self-righteous people who take pride in the spiritual institution to which they affiliate themselves.

I acknowledge God has given humankind a mandate to govern the world. However, legislation must have, as its foundation, deepest love for humanity and exalted reverence for God and His inspired sacred text. Otherwise, man can easily become his own mediator, offering up his good works as a sweet-smelling fragrance to God.

Darker still, there is the potential for our appetite to become our god, measuring our spirituality by our earthly accomplishments through which we bring glory to ourselves as mentioned in Philippians 3:19.

The Apostle Paul explains in Philippians 3:18-19, the mindset of social acceptance is an enemy of the cross of Messiah. Self-gratification is the central priority, an altar that demands homage. The pathway that leads to destruction appears glorious to the world. However, it is shameful in God's sight.

I am a Black man following a Jewish Messiah. However, in the body of Messiah, "the Church", my pigmentation should bear little significance. It is the Church's responsibility to evaluate and determine the authenticity of the depth of my love and knowledge of God. Saints, influenced solely by Holy Spirit, must seek to bridge the cultural divide.

By the same Spirit, the Church, once having identified my God given spiritual gifts, should make room for them to be utilized and appreciated. According to Ephesians 4:8-13, through the proper implementation of the spiritual giftings the Church is equipped for the work of ministry and matured into the full measure of Messiah representation.

It is my prayer that Believers would stop using terminology such as, "I don't see color." Although I understand what is being implied, the reality is that we do see color. I assure you, if the right circumstance presented itself, we would feel the awkwardness of our color differences. In fact, our reaction would more than likely betray our declaration of color blindness.

God's plan is to eradicate the cultural divide. A dilemma having nothing to do with neither gender nor race. It is the unifying of Jew and Gentile, one in Messiah, one new man. This is God's ultimate plan and it should be the platform on which the Christian stands. I believe this is the narrative to which the Christian should devote deep and lengthy contemplation.

DECEIVED OR MASTER MANIPULATOR

What does it look like when a believer has not fully reconciled his cultural preferences with the truth of sacred scripture? It looks like Frank. It looks like Pastor Reggie, and it looks like me.

My eleventh-grade school year was fast coming to its end. I had only been back in Dayton, Ohio for half of the school year. Charlotte, North Carolina had been my home for the former year and a half. My mother, frustrated with my escalating delinquency, sent me to Charlotte to live with my grandmother. Though she never said it, I knew that my mother was afraid for me. She had confronted me on more than one occasion about rumors that I was hanging out with thieves and drug dealers. I left her no choice after a violent confrontation with three older guys in the parking lot of our apartment complex. I remember being in the center of this three-man triangle.

My mother burst onto our porch shouting, "All three of y'all ain't gonna jump on him." One of the guys turned and ordered my mother, "Shut up, bitch". I struck him and pandemonium erupted. With fists flying, my mother and I found ourselves in the middle of a slugfest.

The fight seemed to end as quickly as it started. The three guys backed up, jumped into their car, and spun away. My mother, shocked with tears in her eyes, slapped me. I did not react, which merited another vicious slap. She turned and walked quickly into the apartment. I spent the night at my best friend's place.

A week later, my mother would come to the hospital to pick me up around midnight. I had been in a car accident with two of my friends. The elder of us had stolen a car belonging to his mother's boyfriend. I was high on black beauties, a slang name for an amphetamine housed in a black capsule, I was also heavily intoxicated. Needless to say, I was seriously incoherent.

It seemed as if I was on a bus to Charlotte before I sobered up. My partner in crime, Michael, had managed to slip me a half ounce of weed. I was thankful. Externally, I was angry and uncaring. I showed no emotions to what I interpreted as my mother's rejection of her first born. Internally, I was a broken child. My feelings of rejection seemed to overwhelm me. I cannot remember if I simply lacked the ability to articulate my pain, or if I was too uncomfortable to share my feelings. I internalized them, nonetheless.

I could breathe in Charlotte. I slowly began to drop my guard. However, the things I suppressed afforded me no rest. My pain and confusion found expression through my continued rebellion and my appetite for drugs and violence. Eventually, my mother had no other options, she had to rescue her mother from me. My return to Dayton was bittersweet. Upon my return I met, for the first time, my mother's new husband.

Finally, my mother had gotten out of the inner city. She and this stranger to me had bought a small house in the suburbs. Her husband and I began to clash almost immediately. I felt as if I did not belong there. I missed my grandmother, the gentle way in which she loved me impacted me. She was a perfect example of Messiah-likeness. In my adolescence, I could not articulate what was happening with me. In her eyes I could do no wrong.

For weeks, after my mother brought me back to Dayton, I often drifted off to sleep at nights, just thinking of how my grandmother communicated her love for me. She was not one to use a lot of words, nor do I recall ever seeing my grandmother display affection or become overly emotional. Yet, I felt her love for me. Hundreds of miles away from

Charlotte, North Carolina I could feel her love for me. Years would pass before I realized just how perfect an example of Messiah-likeness my grandmother was.

Somewhere, deep within me, I wanted to live up to the expectations I perceived my grandmother had of me. I wanted to be the young man that she saw when she lovingly looked at me. I just wanted to go back to Charlotte.

These rapid changes had taken a toll on me. While with my grandmother, I had managed to get an after-school job at a local cafeteria and a girlfriend, both of which were new to me. I was slowly changing for the better, but I persisted with my lifestyle of partying. Drugs and alcohol continued to be a big part of my life. I enjoyed the concept of dating a beautiful young lady.

Denise and I were polar opposites. Despite my efforts, I could not reciprocate her faithfulness to me. Nor did her lack of interest in drugs, alcohol and partying have any effect on me. Looking back over our years of marriage, I know it was the grace of God that kept us together. I am very thankful God gave me the perfect helpmeet.

Then Frank entered my life. Frank marked two firsts in my life. He was the first White man and the first Christian I had ever taken the time to listen to. Frank managed a small warehouse. My uncle had gotten me a summer job there. It was the last summer of high school for me. It was hard to believe my twelfth-grade year was fast approaching.

But that reality was overshadowed by my excitement to be back in Charlotte for the summer. I enjoyed working in that warehouse, so much so, that I literally worked circles around the full-time employees. I often spent my lunch break sitting in Frank's office. I would ask him questions about warehousing. He would always find a reason to bring Jesus into the conversation. Frank was a Sunday school teacher at his church. Although I was annoyed by his subtle attempts to offer salvation to me, I did not mind him using me as a sounding board for his lessons.

Before that fateful summer, while in Dayton one of the art teachers had taken an interest in my talent. He and some other faculty had mapped out a course of action that would secure a scholarship for me. I would have to come to school an hour before school started and stay an hour late. I would have to do this for most of my twelfth-grade year. Although the idea of me actually becoming someone other than what my environment dictated excited me, deep down within I was terrified. So, when Frank presented me with the idea of staying on at the warehouse, using it as a stepping stone to a career in warehousing, I jumped at the opportunity. "You can go to night school and get your GED," Frank enthusiastically said.

I did not hesitate. Smiling from ear to ear, I sealed my fate. I received no encouragement to turn the offer down to pursue a career in the visual arts. My mother, my uncle, not even my grandmother gave a hint that the road I was embarking on would prove to be a dead end.

Over and over again, I trained White guys and high school graduates to be my managers. I grew to hate my job, to hate White people more and more with each passing year. In the midst of all that hatred, I began to hate myself.

There is no darker place on earth than to arrive at that place of despising self. That place where cowardice is the only thing standing between you and suicide. This Jewish Messiah was waiting there for me. Waiting for me to ask for His help. Waiting, not just to point me in the direction of, but to lead me, guide, and comfort me over the challenging mountains, through the vast valleys to my God ordained destiny. The place that God had preordained for me to stand before the foundations of the earth.

I walked into Frank's office holding an invoice while my head was down, my eyes studying a discrepancy in the numbers. "Frank, it looks like this inbound is short." I began explaining while slowly raising my eyes up from the invoice. A brief moment of silence gripped me. Frank sat behind his desk, his hair was disheveled, head in his hands. I alarmingly asked, "Damn man, what the hell is wrong with you?"

Frank exhaustingly lifted his head up. It was obvious, he had been crying. I quickly grew uncomfortable; I had never seen a grown man cry. I wanted to escape, but just as I was about to turn away, Frank began to explain his dilemma. If he had just looked up at me, I know my awkward facial expression would have silenced him.

I vividly remember that day. Frank belted out, "Ronnie's not going to college!" His voice cracked; his eyes scanned the room as if he were lost. "He wants to marry that girl," Frank continued, his face distorted with anger. "I told him he was throwing his life away," he added in a snarling whisper. Frank put his head back into his hands.

Frank never acknowledged my presence. I stood there, staring at this broken man. He was mourning a decision his son had made, while I was steaming over the hypocrisy he displayed. My frustration ignited into full blown hatred. It was a devastating reality check. I struggled to repress the feelings of betrayal and heartbreak I was experiencing in that moment.

I stood there, numb in the doorway to his office. A thousand responses danced inside my head like boiling water. For a moment, I was paralyzed. I felt nothing, not one remorseful thought. I said to myself, "this cracker sat there in that same seat and counseled me to drop out of high school!"

I thought, "so this was the White man's Christianity, just another one of his weapons of oppression." In that moment, I became obnoxiously racist.

I wanted White people to know that I was fully conscious of their evil desire to destroy the Black man. I was totally void of even a consoling word. Slowly, I turned my back to him and walked out.

Christianity is garbage, I remember thinking as I walked back onto the dock. I signed the driver's invoice, got on my forklift, took the emergency brake off, put it in gear and proceeded to drive back into the warehouse. Neither I nor the truck driver said anything about the boxes that he was missing. He did not want to fill out a short-shipped form, and I just did not care. I was numb. Christianity was a joke. Apart from my grandmother, Christians were cartoon characters, smiling deviants. They were silk tongued hypocrites, ready to rip your heart out at the opportune moment. These were the thoughts that hauntingly lingered in my mind.

I was seventeen years old, and I had seen nothing attractive about Christianity. In my ignorance I thought this Caucasian Jesus would never favor me. And why should He, even my own people saw my darker complexion as a condition to be mocked. I had no idea that I was strategically being moved further and further away from my God ordained destiny.

The day would come when my eyes would be opened to the beauty and power of this glorious gospel. The day would come, when I would personally experience the life changing impact of arriving at the knowledge of the truth.

The day would come, when the humility of brokenness, the humbling of despair, and sorrow's torment would bring me to that place of sweet surrender to Holy Spirit's leadership.

Unfortunately, my encounter with Frank was not the only time I felt deceived. I met Pastor Reggie while serving time in a minimum-security prison camp. He looked like a young Clint Eastwood, tall, handsome, and charismatic. The fourth Sunday evening of every month Pastor Reggie would lead his team of volunteers into a small recreation building filled with predominantly Black inmates. His sermons, though always entertaining, were powerfully convicting.

Month after month, Pastor Reggie passionately communicated God's displeasure with sin. Lust, fornication, pride and coveting, these nasty offenses always found their way into the fabric of his sermons. Pastor Reggie's desire to see us live godly lives was authentic. However, in retrospect, I cannot recall him ever expressing God's love for us. Although I had experienced God's unwavering love for me, I had yet to recognize it as the single most critical component in attracting the seemingly unlovable.

Prison is a multicultural environment. Gang culture, religious culture, and various ethnic cultures, they all co-exist within the confines of a few miles of barbed wire and massive steel fencing. I chose the Christian culture.

However, in hindsight, I recognize the prompting of God's intervening hand. In my increasing zeal for God and the Bible, I discovered the beauty and power of discipline. My days consisted of prayer, searching the Scriptures, witnessing, and discipling. Jogging around the fence, and lifting weights became a significant part of my routine as well.

I worked hard at displaying Jesus' courage and His love as I considered these attributes His most important. It was these character traits that earned me the respect of those incarcerated with me, as well as the volunteers and officers.

The State of North Carolina has a unique sponsorship program. It allows qualifying volunteers to take inmates out on six-hour passes. It was designed to help inmates' transition back into society. Pastor Reggie used it to quickly establish himself as a mentor to me. I was excited about going out on pass with Pastor Reggie.

It was a short-lived relationship.

I had been out with several volunteers, but this would be my first time going out with a pastor. I had passionately embraced the role of spiritual leader at the Camp Green minimal custody prison. So, I deemed this opportunity to spend one on one time with a pastor as a necessary experience.

I met Pastor Reggie at the main gate Sunday morning, I approached the guard shack as Pastor Reggie was signing me out. "You good to go Graves," the officer said as he stepped aside, allowing me to walk out of the gate. Dressed in a suit and tie, clutching my Bible close to my chest with one hand, I extended my right hand and firmly shook Pastor Reggie's hand.

I felt important. We arrived at church about an hour before the service. Within the twenty-minute drive, from the camp to the church, Pastor Reggie drilled me on the responsibilities of a pastor. I was in mentee's heaven.

The service was about an hour and a half long. It was my first encounter with an entirely White congregation. The inner-city equips you with certain survival techniques. The inherent instinct of reading people is essential. I developed assessing facial expressions and body posture into a knee jerk reaction. I sat in the empty sanctuary observing members as they trickled in. I received awkward smiles from some. Others, preoccupied with greeting their fellow Church members, ignored me altogether.

Some even seemed uncomfortable with my presence. At the end of the service, Pastor Reggie introduced me as Morris, visiting from the prison camp. Following his introduction, many came up to greet me. I was extremely uncomfortable. I did my best to conceal my feelings of being unwelcomed. I repeatedly reprimanded myself. I was prejudging my heart against God-fearing saints. Silently, I prayed that my smile would appear authentic.

Later in Pastor Reggie's home, sitting at his dinner table, joined by his wife and two sons. Pastor Reggie gave credence to the things that I had been feeling. One of his sons had captured a large Velvet ant. He handed me the jar containing the hairy, yellow, and black creature. "This thing looks like a wasp without wings," I said. "I know!" His son replied and proceeded to excitedly explain how he had found it in their backyard. Suddenly, out of nowhere Pastor Reggie interjected, "God does not condone the mixing of races." Pastor Reggie proceeded to give Bible verses to substantiate his statement. My initial thought was, "Where did that come from?"

As Pastor Reggie continued to make his case, I pondered on his verbal presentation. I stared studiously. His eyes revealed the sincerity of his conviction. I had given the last four and a half years of my life to reading and studying the sacred scriptures.

I knew this man was either deceived, or he was a master manipulator. The subject closed with my simple reply, "I disagree." I gave no reference, nor did he ask me to elaborate further.

At that moment, I knew his heart. I determined those that followed his teachings had to harbor the same feelings. After that evening, Pastor Reggie's assistant pastor took over his prison ministry. It would be years before I would see Pastor Reggie again.

Eventually, Holy Spirit opened my spiritual eyes to the reality of the true deceiver, the master manipulator. He is a created being; his blazing envy of God drove him into the depths of self-deception. Lucifer, a radiantly beautiful angel and worshiper.

He desired the one seat in glory that he could never occupy. His contemplations of a coup cost him and a third of the angelic host to be banished from their positions in glory. These fallen angels despise God. They will do anything within their power to strike a blow to the heart of God.

Their strategy is to consistently challenge you to question the legitimacy of God's love for you. Fallen angels are spirit beings. This means, they cannot personally interact with a natural or carnal being.

Therefore, they must rely on nouns, people, places, and things. Our Messiah understood this, when Peter attempted to encourage Him to abandon the course God had set before him. Yeshua had the insight to address the one influencing Peter.

I have walked with Holy Spirit now for half of my life. The irony is, at various stages of my journey, I have been some version of the child tormenting preacher, I have been Pastor Reggie, and even Frank. I think the most important thing I have learned is to remember the man in the mirror, what manner of man I am, James 1:23-24.

What manner of man do I desire to be? Better still, do those that I encounter, behold the image of

Messiah in my language and conduct? If they do not, then I could very well be deceived by the master manipulator. The question is never, "can we be deceived?" but rather, "how easily are we deceived?"

"And the great dragon was thrown down, the serpent of old who is called the devil and Satan, who deceives the whole world; he was thrown down to the earth, and his angels were thrown down with him," Revelation 12:9.

The painful truth about being manipulated; controlled or influenced; (a person or situation) cleverly, unfairly, or unscrupulously; taken advantage of, is not that people can be manipulated, but rather, how difficult it is to convince people of the truth once they have been.

THE OPINIONS OF THOSE
FOLLOWING A JEWISH MESSIAH

Michelle Wright's opinion concerning following a Jewish Messiah as a Black woman:

"Since there is and has been a racial divide for years, I don't know how, or even if the church can respond to the resolution of the racial divide as it relates to the historical mistreatment of Black Americans.

In recent conversation, many non-Black respondents have simply said, "they are unsure of what should be said, or even what can be said or done that would help with racial reconciliation." Reasoning, they cannot relate or understand our experiences; therefore, they say nothing.

However, at the very base and foundation of our church experience we have, or should have been taught the differences between the simple concepts of right versus wrong, good versus evil, light versus darkness, love versus hate. These teachings, I'm pretty sure are understood by all. That God created us all and we all are created in His image. When God looked at all He had made, He said, "it was very good," (Genesis 1:31).

So, I honestly struggle with the responses, or lack of responses from other people to these simple concepts. I now believe and have come to the understanding that if these biblical, simple and foundational concepts are not understood as well as applied, then it is a stony-heart issue.

Love is inborn and innate. Racial division is taught. Unless or until a person comes into agreement with the simple biblical concepts as well as open to change, open to learn, open to understanding and accepting differences, it is my belief the church alone can do nothing concerning racial reconciliation."

Wade McHargue's opinion concerning following a Jewish Messiah as a Caucasian man:

"Even though as a Caucasian, I grew up in a community where many of my friends were African American. I was baptized in an African American church (going down into the waters to the songs of negro spirituals). My best man in my wedding was African American. Furthermore, having lived in Africa for seven years, I have come to recognize my experience has been far different than many others.

It was testimonies like Morris' that opened my eyes more to what many African Americans have faced, not only in their lives, but generationally. It was the

Lord's challenge to me to listen and try to put myself in my brother Morris' shoes. In addition, the challenge was so I would better understand what African Americans faced, even today in 2020 at the time of this writing. The Lord challenged me to try and feel some of their pain, frustration and justified anger.

Secondly, in trying to feel the pain and emotion of what they've gone through, it made me respect brothers like Morris even more because I see how they have overcome so much in life as they walked in enormous grace and love. I'm convicted by the love I see in them.

A love that is proven by refusing hate to settle in their hearts. A love that is willing to not only trust again, but to embrace, befriend, as well as show the character of Messiah to those that have broken that trust, being a racist hypocrite. I think of C.S. Lewis's quote, "We can ignore even pleasure, but pain insists upon being attended to. God whispers to us in our pleasures, speaks in our conscience, but shouts in our pains; it is His megaphone to rouse a deaf world."

I believe a lot of White people are deaf, and have not listened intently enough to the pain of our

African American brothers. However, if they will, they will find themselves attending to this wound and stop pretending it doesn't exist. As Morris knows, and lives, the culture of the Kingdom overrides all other cultures. That culture is one of humility, love, and preferring others better than oneself.

I'm challenged and humbled by the life along with the testimony of Morris as well as those like him. For it is in the face of self-righteousness, pride, racism, lack of compassion that the character of Jesus is shown most beautifully and profoundly as the truths of Yeshua's words are lived out,

"You have heard that it was said, 'You shall love your neighbor and hate your enemy.' But I say to you, love your enemies, bless those who curse you, do good to those who hate you, and pray for those who spitefully use you and persecute you, that you may be sons of your Father in heaven; for He makes His sun rise on the evil and on the good, and sends rain on the just and on the unjust.

For if you love those who love you, what reward have you? Do not even the tax collectors do the same? And if you greet your brethren only, what do you do more than others? Do not even the tax collectors do so? Therefore, you shall be perfect, just as your Father in heaven is perfect." (Matthew 5:43-48, emphasis mine). This changed the world in Yeshua's day of walking the earth, and it will change today's world as well. May we be those channels of His divine love, truth and grace."

Harry Kaufmann's opinion concerning following a Jewish Messiah.

"Black, White and Church, is really about identity, not the building. Church is about identity. Once you are born again, you are a dead man. You can get stuck in the race problems of your day, or focus on certain parts of history, but you can't change the fact that you are a dead man, crucified in Jesus, raised up in Jesus and glorified in Jesus.

Now you are a son or daughter of the Most High God. Identity. Unfortunately, you must also act like it. With inheritance as well as authority comes responsibility and accountability. Oops! Are you still begging for something you want or need from God? Better rethink that. Or did you just sign on for Heaven and eternity apart from Hell without the inconvenience of living out your restored relationship with the Father while you are temporarily on earth?

What does honor your father and mother mean now? Maybe being seated with Jesus at the right hand of the Father isn't such a good thing. Father God might start asking questions about how you are doing things.

If Jesus is the head, what about His body? That's you church. Take a look in the mirror. What do you see? No use kidding yourself. The Holy Spirit knows every freckle and He won't settle for a spot or blemish.

What about Blacks, Whites, tribes, tongues, and nations in church? It is diverse, and it's also family. It is a glimpse of where we are going. It is salt and light for where we are now."

MY CONCLUSION

Everything that has touched and influenced my life, God allowed it. He is all knowing, He is all powerful, and in His divine sovereignty, God has given man the tremendous responsibility of governing his own will. What does this mean to me? As a Black man following a Jewish Messiah, it means, I have abandoned my own will, that I might entirely embrace God's will for my life.

I believe the things God has permitted to impact my life He can use to bring glory to His great name. My responsibility is to consistently choose to respond to every circumstance as if God is watching, waiting for me to refuse to execute my will, in expectation of experiencing the destiny He has pre-ordained for me.

As Joseph explained to his brothers, the things they perpetrated against him, were birthed out of evil intentions. God foreseen it and incorporated it into His divine plan for Joseph's life. Unlike his brothers, Joseph had a deep desire to be well-pleasing to his father, Jacob. This meant that he was heavily influenced by his grandfather, Abraham, who was totally influenced and submitted to God. In the life of Joseph, I see that a man does not have to succumb to repeated exposure to evil events that threaten to callus the heart.

MY CONCLUSION

My Blackness, the culture that molded my approach to life, the events that shaped my worldview, of which, I have only shared a fraction with you, prove that I was well on my way to becoming a bitter man.

Did I become bitter? I submit to you that I evolved. I abandoned the brokenness of my culture, yet I embraced the uniqueness afforded to me by God through my culture. Yeshua Messiah did not abandon His culture. He challenged it. He confronted the norms of His day, and He embraced the outcasts of which I was one.

ABOUT THE AUTHOR

Morris Graves, Jr. is a Pastor, Bible Teacher, and Author. He is the Lead Pastor of Christ Discipleship Ministry a nonprofit organization where he teaches, mentors and disciples' other believers to hear the Holy Spirit for themselves.

Affectionately known as Pastor Morris, he has served in ministry for over 30 years. The last 12 years, as of the date of this publication, with Sid Roth's *It's Supernatural!* and Messianic Vision headquartered in Charlotte, North Carolina. Pastor Morris is one of three pastors ordained by Sid Roth. Morris is an on staff Pastor, serving as a relationship builder in the Partner Relations department.

Pastor Morris has also been active in many other roles with Sid Roth's *It's Supernatural!* and Messianic Vision, such as, working in production, interviewing guests for the "There Must Be Something More Show."

He is the host of, "Your Mentoring Moment With Pastor Morris," which is a live morning show that airs worldwide on the It's Supernatural Network (ISN). In addition, the same show airs as a podcast on the Spotify platform. Pastor Morris has been interviewed by Sid Roth on *It's Supernatural!* He has also been a guest on "There Must Be Something More," once by himself and again with his daughter sharing their testimonies.

Pastor Morris also served as a bridge Ministry Pastor at Steele Creek Church of Charlotte, a multiethnic church under Senior Lead Pastor Kelvin Smith for eight years. While serving at Steele Creek, he founded their Prison Ministry and led it for nine years.

Pastor Morris and his precious wife, Emma Denise Graves have been married since 1981. They are the proud parents of two lovely children, daughter JaCynthia Bailey and son, Morris Justin Graves. They have four beautiful grandchildren and love spending time with their family. Pastor Morris and Emma are dedicated servants of the Lord Jesus Christ. They both desire for others to hear from God and go out in the world fulfilling the call on their lives.

For more information, please visit
www.morrisgravesjr.com.

You can find many of Pastor Morris' teachings with the Christ Discipleship Ministry on his YouTube Channel at Morris Graves Jr.